WOMEN AND WAR

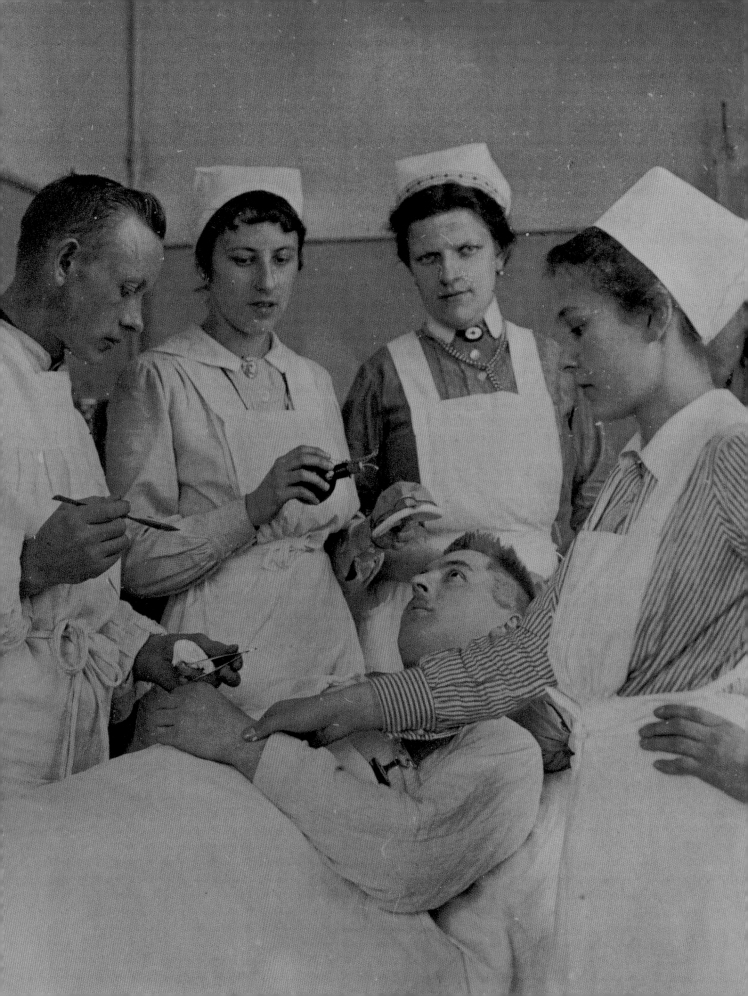

WOMEN AND WAR

ANN KRAMER

FRANKLIN WATTS
LONDON·SYDNEY

Designer Thomas Keenes
Editor Sarah Ridley
Art Director Jonathan Hair
Editor-in-Chief John C. Miles
Picture Research Diana Morris

First published in 2004
by Franklin Watts
96 Leonard Street
London
EC2A 4XD

Franklin Watts Australia
45-51 Huntley Street
Alexandria
NSW 2015

ISBN 0 7496 5156 3

A CIP catalogue record for this book
is available from the British Library.

Printed in Malaysia

Picture credits

AKG Images: front and back cover
background, 2, 10b, 17t
IWM/TRH Pictures: 13t
Peter Newark's Pictures: 7, 9, 23t,
27t, 29b
Slava Katamidze Collection/Hulton
Archive: 21b
Topham Picturepoint: 15b, 19b, 24b

*Every attempt has been made to clear
copyright. Should there be any inadvertent
omission, please apply to the publisher for
rectification.*

CONTENTS

ON THE EVE OF WAR

In 1914 the lives of women were very restricted. Some women were employed outside the home, but only a few jobs were considered suitable. Very few women had the vote. World War One would bring many changes.

WORKING WOMEN

Before the war, most working-class women worked for a living. In Britain, for example, more than five million women were working for a wage. They worked in factories, particularly textile factories, in offices and in shops. Many women – more than two million in Britain – worked as domestic servants. In France, Germany and Russia, which were less industrialised than Britain, millions of women also worked on the land.

However, women earned much less than men. Also, society divided jobs into those considered suitable for men and for women. Skilled trades involving long training were considered to be "men's work".

After years of campaigning for equal rights, women had made some advances. Even so, they were still second-class citizens. Most women were dependent on men. A woman's place was still considered to be in the home. Married women were not supposed to do paid work. Middle-class women were expected to stay at home, look after the family and run the household. Some women challenged convention but they were rare.

FEMINISM AND THE VOTE

Some feminists had been fighting for the vote for many years, but by 1914 the only places where women could vote were Finland, Norway, New Zealand, parts of Australia and a few American states. Elsewhere women could not vote or take part in government.

British feminists were active and well organised and by 1913 their campaign had become extremely militant. It was spearheaded by Emmeline and Christabel Pankhurst, leaders of the Women's Social and Political

Women's Suffrage
Feminist activity before 1914
1869 Women in Wyoming, USA, gain the vote.
1893 New Zealand women gain the vote.
1897 National Union of Women's Suffrage Societies (NUWSS) is formed in Britain. Millicent Fawcett is president.
1902 International Women's Suffrage Alliance (IWSA) is founded.
1903 Pankhursts launch Women's Social and Political Union (WSPU) in Britain.
1904 IWSA holds first international congress, Berlin, Germany. It continues to meet every year until 1914.
1905 Christabel Pankhurst and Annie Kenney are arrested and imprisoned for heckling at a political meeting.
1906 Women in Finland gain the vote.
1908 Icelandic Women's Association is founded.
1908 Australian women gain the vote.
1909 First British suffragette goes on hunger strike in prison.
1909 International Women's Day begins in the USA.
1911 Around 60,000 suffragettes demonstrate in London.
1912 Police raid WSPU headquarters. Leadership arrested.
1913 Norwegian women gain the vote.

Mrs Emmeline Pankhurst, the suffragette leader, arrested outside Buckingham Palace while trying to present a petition to the king, 21 May 1914.

"... Let us prove ourselves worthy of citizenship whether our claim [the vote] is recognised or not."

Millicent Fawcett,
Common Cause, 1914

Union (WSPU). Known as suffragettes, members of the WSPU had been confronting the government since 1905 in their attempt to win the vote. Many had been imprisoned; some had died.

American women had held the first ever women's rights conference as far back as 1848. They tried to win the vote state by state. But by 1910 women had the vote only in Wyoming, Utah, Colorado and Idaho. Leading feminists increasingly looked to WSPU tactics to bring about changes.

By 1914 feminists from different countries were working together through the International Women's Suffrage Alliance (IWSA). Some, because of their campaigning experience, were well placed to respond to the demands of the coming war.

WAR BREAKS OUT

World War One began on 4 August 1914. Thousands of men left to fight. Women too responded with patriotic enthusiasm, offering their help. But it would be some time before their skills were fully utilised.

IMMEDIATE IMPACT

War had an immediate impact on women's lives. In Britain, some 250,000 men joined up in the first month alone. Wives, mothers and daughters were left behind, without the main breadwinner. Governments introduced separation allowances for wives whose husbands had gone to fight.

Many women were thrown out of work. Trade was hit and wealthy families cut back on domestic servants. Many working-class women experienced real poverty. Women such as Sylvia Pankhurst set up charities to help. The British government introduced the Defence of the Realm Act (DORA) which put industry on to a war footing and gradually many women were absorbed into war work.

HELPING THE WAR EFFORT

Middle- and upper-class women rallied to help the war effort. Some donned uniforms and set up military-style voluntary organisations. Others knitted, raised money for medical supplies, provided comforts for the troops and housed refugees made homeless by the war.

RECRUITMENT AND PROPAGANDA

Fighting on the Western Front soon settled into relentless trench warfare. As casualties mounted, increasing numbers of men were needed to fight.

Women – directly and indirectly – were used for propaganda. Posters showed images of "ideal" wives and mothers encouraging men to join up. Rumours of attacks on women and children were used to foster anti-German feeling and stimulate more recruitment.

"On August 4, 1914, the door of the Doll's House opened. For the shot that was fired in Serbia summoned men to their most ancient occupation – and women to every other."

Mabel Potter Dagget, American journalist

VERA BRITTAIN

VERA BRITTAIN (1893-1970) was a British writer and feminist. Born into a middle-class family, she studied at Oxford University. When war broke out, she wrote in her diary that she had started "knitting... the only work it seems possible yet for women to do." She soon joined the Voluntary Aid Detachment (VAD) as a nurse and served in France.

The conditions she saw and her own personal losses made her a pacifist. Her diary was published as *Testament of Youth*. It has become a classic account of one woman's experience of World War One.

This recruiting poster shows "ideal" women encouraging men to go and fight.

Some women actively encouraged men to fight. Emmeline Pankhurst, for instance, gave white feathers as a symbol of cowardice to men who were not in uniform. However, many women attacked this campaign as shameful.

DIVISIONS

In Britain, and elsewhere, war split the women's movement. Emmeline Pankhurst ended suffragette activity and offered support to the government. By 1915 she and many other suffrage leaders were demanding the right to be involved. However, some feminists were opposed to the war and campaigned against it.

☛ VOLUNTARY WORK

Women on both sides did unpaid work to help servicemen's families, civilians displaced by war and soldiers.

◆ In England, Austria, France and Russia voluntary organisations aided refugees. They took them into their homes and provided food, clothes and other help.

◆ In Austria, Jewish women gave help to Jewish refugees fleeing from Galicia. They provided money, soup kitchens, schools and clinics.

◆ German women, including many middle-class feminists, formed local associations to help the needy. They set up soup kitchens and crèches.

◆ Women throughout Europe and in North America organised to help soldiers. They provided comforts such as knitted socks and parcels of food, cigarettes and treats.

◆ In Ireland, 300 women knitted 20,000 pairs of socks and 10,000 scarves for servicemen.

◆ In Australia and New Zealand women formed patriotic clubs and societies to provide comforts for soldiers.

◆ In France, Britain and Germany women set up canteens at train stations and provided tea, cigarettes and soup for soldiers.

◆ Some Frenchwomen, known as *marraines* (godmothers) "adopted" a soldier as a *filleul* (godson) and sent him letters and treats.

TO THE FRONT

Thousands of women around the world signed up to nurse wounded soldiers.
Some were professional nurses. Others were untrained volunteers.
Nursing brought them face to face with the horrors of war.

AT HOME AND ABROAD

Thanks to the work of women such as Florence Nightingale, military nursing was considered a suitable job for a woman to do. Women from Britain, Russia, France, Germany and other countries flocked to nurse sick, wounded and dying men. Some worked in hospitals at home, receiving wounded soldiers streaming in from ambulance trains and ships. Others worked in field hospitals near the battlefields.

"Some of these new patients have dreadful, dreadful wounds. One young boy with part of his face shot away, both arms gone and great wounds in both legs..."

Clare Gass,
Canadian nurse,
7 June 1915

A casualty is treated by nurses and a doctor in a German hospital in May 1917.

VOLUNTEERS

Professional nurses were enlisted immediately, while thousands of other women volunteered. In Britain most joined the Voluntary Aid Detachments (VADs). VADs had to buy their own uniforms and, until 1916, were unpaid. They trained for about three months.

Nurses were not meant to work close to the front line: Russian nurses were supposed to stay in mobile field hospitals and the French Medical Service barred women from the battlefield. Very soon, however, nurses worked in field hospitals close to the fighting. Two British women, Elsie Knocker and Mairi Chisholm, known as the "women of Pervyse", worked under fire.

Women travelled great distances to nurse, coming from the United States (as early as 1914, before the USA entered the war), Canada, Australia and New Zealand.

HORRIFIC CASUALTIES

Nothing had prepared nurses or doctors for the dreadful conditions and the enormous numbers of casualties, particularly following the Battle of the Somme in 1916. Tents and abandoned buildings such as churches were used as field hospitals; here nurses worked long hours in crude operating theatres. During heavy fighting, there might be more than four operations going on simultaneously. The only painkillers were aspirin and morphine. There were no antibiotics to cope with infections and the smell of gangrene could be overpowering.

Despite their horrific wounds, soldiers appreciated the careful nursing provided by women who rarely slept during a "big push". Many nurses wrote of their sadness when men whom they had nursed back to health had to go back into the living hell of the trenches.

FACING DANGERS

Medical personnel risked shelling and bombardment. In May 1918 the British and Canadian hospitals at Étaples were bombed. Nurses were among the dead and wounded. In June an Allied hospital ship was sunk. The dead included 14 Canadian nurses. Nurses also suffered dysentery, cholera and influenza, to say nothing of sheer exhaustion.

☛ NURSING STATISTICS

Thousands of women from many countries worked as nurses during World War One. Exact figures are difficult to find, but these give an idea:

- France: approximately 30,000 temporary military nurses and 60,000 Red Cross nurses.
- Germany: approximately 92,000 nurses and aides. They worked on the Western and Eastern Fronts.
- Britain: 15,165 trained nurses and 12,501 partially trained or untrained nurses (including 1,685 VADs working for the Royal Medical Corps in 1918).
- Ireland: about 4,500 VADs.
- New Zealand: approximately 650.
- Australia: about 2,500.
- United States: more than 21,840 nurses in the Army Nurse Corps (ANC) and Army Nurses and 1,386 in the Navy Nurse Corps. For the first time black American nurses were enrolled. Some 4,600 Red Cross nurses, of whom 1,800 were black.

MARIE CURIE

MARIE CURIE (1867-1934) was a brilliant Polish chemist who discovered radium. During World War One, she and her daughter Irene volunteered to X-ray wounded soldiers on the front. Together they visited over 300 field hospitals in France and Belgium, teaching military surgeons how to find bullets and shrapnel in soldiers' wounds. They also trained X-ray technicians. Travelling in vans, nicknamed *"Petits Curies"*, Mme Curie and her daughter took essential radiological equipment to all the major battle areas, including Amiens, Ypres and Verdun.

WOMEN DOCTORS

Some women had qualified as doctors before 1914. When war began, they offered their help. Governments and the male-dominated military did not welcome women doctors in the same way as nurses. So some female doctors made their own way to the front.

TAKING THE INITIATIVE

At the outbreak of war, Dr Elsie Inglis, a distinguished doctor and Scottish suffragist, suggested that women's medical units should serve on the Western Front. The War Office told her to "go home and sit still". This was not unusual. Many women doctors who wanted to serve abroad had to use their own initiative. They funded, organised and set up medical units, finding their own way to where they were needed.

SCOTTISH WOMEN'S HOSPITALS

With money raised by the National Union of Women's Suffrage Societies (NUWSS) and the American Red Cross, Dr Inglis set up the Scottish Women's Hospitals (SWH). Because the British War Office did not want her workforce, Dr Inglis offered her services to other Allied governments, particularly Serbia. By 1918 there were 14 Scottish women's medical units in France, Serbia, Corsica, Salonika, Romania, Russia and Malta.

WIDER OPPORTUNITIES

It was often easier for women doctors to help the war effort at home. As male doctors left for the Western Front, women took over as hospital doctors. Women were also encouraged to enter medical schools, which had previously been closed to them.

In 1915 the British War Office gave Doctors Louisa Garrett Anderson and Flora Murray permission to set up the Endell Street Military Hospital in London. By the time it closed in 1919, it had treated some 26,000 patients.

GERTRUDE STEIN

GERTRUDE STEIN (1874-1946) was an American writer. Between June 1917 and March 1918 she was a driver with the American Fund for French Wounded, an organisation of women volunteers who operated a car fleet in France, which was used to carry displaced families and wounded to safety. Caught up in the German counter-offensive, she and others then went on to operate mobile canteens and aid centres.

After the war, she settled in Paris. Disillusioned with war and American society, she famously described herself and other disenchanted writers as the "Lost Generation".

"Dying men lay huddled so closely together on the floor that they touched each other. Blood and pus oozed from the wounds."

Dr Isobel Hutton, Royaumont Abbey Hospital, France

A FANY ambulance driver poses beside her vehicle in 1918.

1914

August Evelina Haverfield founds the Women's Emergency Corps. It helps organise women to serve as doctors, nurses and motorcycle messengers at the front.

August Dr Hector Munro's Flying Ambulance Corps goes to Belgium with Elsie Knocker and Mairi Chisholm.

November Elsie Knocker and Mairi Chisholm set up a first-aid post at Pervyse, Belgium.

1915

January Dr Eleanor Soltau sets up the first Scottish Women's Hospital Unit in Serbia.

February Endell Street Military Hospital opens in London; the first to be staffed entirely by women.

October–December Serbian Army and members of the Scottish Women's Hospital Unit are forced to retreat over mountains in Albania. Dr Elsie Inglis is captured by Austrians, but repatriated.

1916

1 July Battle of the Somme begins. Massive casualties result. British casualties in one day alone are about 60,000 – a world record.

August London Suffrage Society finances Dr Inglis and 80 women to help Serbian soldiers fighting in Russia.

1917

Elsie Knocker and Mairi Chisholm are awarded the British Military Medal for rescuing a British pilot from no-man's-land.

AMERICAN WOMEN'S HOSPITALS

In 1915 some 9,000 American women were qualified physicians and surgeons. In 1917, when the USA entered the war, many offered their services to the military medical corps. They were refused. The War Service Committee of the Medical Woman's National Association set up their own American Women's Hospitals in Europe. They were staffed entirely by women, including 390 women doctors. Other American women served with the Red Cross, or freelanced.

AMBULANCE DRIVERS

Women also served as orderlies and ambulance drivers. One well-known group was the First-Aid Nursing Yeomanry (FANYs). They were privileged women who worked at the front line driving ambulances, delivering dispatches and setting up troop canteens. They nicknamed themselves "First Anywheres" and delighted in their dangerous work.

WORKING WOMEN

Between 1914 and 1918 women joined the workforce as never before. Whereas before they been employed in factories and offices, on farms and as domestic servants, they now entered work previously only done by men.

EARLY PHASES

At first, women took over the jobs left by their men. Within the first six months of the war, women were cleaning windows, sweeping chimneys, delivering milk and driving carts or wagons, digging graves and driving hearses. By late 1915 in Germany, 14,000 women were working on trams. Twenty per cent of them were married to men who had been enlisted into the army.

MOBILISING WOMEN

As war dragged on and casualties mounted, increasing numbers of men were poured into the trenches. Women workers were needed to replace them on the "home front" and so from 1915 women were actively mobilised for work. In Britain Christabel Pankhurst and the Women's Social and Political Union (WSPU) helped this process by demanding women's right to serve. This demand was backed by politicians.

In 1916 the government of Britain introduced conscription (compulsory enlistment into the services). As male workers left for the front, the drive to recruit women intensified. From 1915, France, too, recruited women for war work. Some German feminists also urged their government to recruit women.

TYPES OF WORK

Women did virtually everything that men had done. Women in Britain, France, Germany, Austria and North America entered the chemical and metalworking industries. They worked in munitions factories, built aircraft and worked in construction. They were employed in communications and as police.

1914

August Central Committee on Women's Employment co-ordinates use of women to replace men in the labour force in Britain.

1915

Women's Auxiliary Force is set up to find part-time work for women with families.

February Women's Police Service is formed in Britain.

March British government draws up a register of women who want to do farming, industrial and clerical work.

May Manchester suffragists form the Women's War Interests Committee to oversee women's conditions in munitions factories.

May Women textile homeworkers receive the minimum wage in France.

July Women's "Right to Serve" demonstration takes place in London.

November Crèches set up in factories in Britain.

1917

Women trained as welfare supervisors in France.

1918

Women transport workers strike for equal wages in Britain. They receive a pay bonus but not equal wages.

More women entered the transport industries than ever before. In Britain in 1914, around 12,000 women worked in transport, but by 1918 numbers had increased to 61,000. Women worked on trains as ticket collectors and guards and drove buses and trams. Women also worked in banking and the postal services.

DIFFICULTIES

Many newspapers and organisations praised women's wartime work. But there was also opposition to employing women in what had been seen as men's jobs. Male trade unions were hostile. They thought women would steal jobs or undercut wages. The public could be critical, too, because it was feared that women would abandon their roles as wives and mothers.

For working-class women war work meant higher wages and greater opportunities. Many left low-paid work for better jobs. Nevertheless, women were still paid less than men and working conditions were often harsh. Later in the war, some crèches and child-care facilities were provided, but most married women had to combine waged work with looking after their home and children. In spite of this, war work gave women not only an income but also the satisfaction of doing what they saw as their duty for the war effort.

A woman conductor issues tickets on the top deck of a bus.

"The woman bus-conductor is a sign of the days which have seen women engaging in every kind of employment..."

Kathleen Courlander

MUNITIONS WORKERS

From 1915 governments called on women to enter munitions factories to make
the huge numbers of guns and shells needed for war. By 1918
thousands of women – married and single – were working in factories.

MUNITIONS WORK

By 1915 the demand for weapons was outstripping
production and the British and German governments
moved industry on to a war footing. As skilled men left
for the front, it became obvious that women would have
to replace them. Britain set up a Ministry of Munitions
and recruited women.

Thousands of women entered the munitions factories,
but male trade unions remained resistant. To overcome
this, governments and unions made a series of deals.
Governments promised that women would only be
employed for the duration of the war. When the men
returned, they would get their jobs back. Finally, unions
agreed to "dilution". This meant that a skilled man's job
was to be split up, or "diluted" between a number of
women workers. In this way, men kept their status as
skilled workers.

Most women who worked in munitions were
members of the working class. They carried out a range
of tasks from running machines through to welding.
They made and filled shells and cartridges and did
heavy labour and cleaning. Within a short space of time,
they proved they could do the work just as well as men.

LONG HOURS

Press and government propaganda portrayed women
munitions workers as heroines. But working conditions
in the factories were difficult and dangerous.

Before 1914 laws limited the number of hours that
people could work in factories, for safety reasons. Now
they were suspended. Women worked 10- or 12-hour
shifts or even longer, often on their feet the whole time.

*"All our front hair was
bright ginger and all
our faces were bright
yellow. They used to
call us canaries."*

Caroline Rennles, munitions worker

MARY MACARTHUR

MARY MACARTHUR (1880-1921)
was a Scottish trade unionist
who fought for better working
conditions for women workers. In
1903 she became secretary of the
Women's Trade Union League. In
1906, with Margaret Bondfield, she
co-founded the National Federation
of Women Workers.

During the war, she campaigned
for better conditions for women in the
munitions factories. She represented
women workers on the Central
Munitions Labour Supply Committee
and the Health of Munitions Workers
Committee. She helped to set up
training and a minimum wage for
women.

Women workers fill shells with explosives at a munitions factory.

DANGEROUS WORK

There were few safety precautions, particularly when the demand for shells was intense. Accidents were common; in France, thousands of women suffered industrial injuries. Conditions in Italian and Russian factories were particularly bad. The risk of explosions was high. Munitions workers also suffered from TNT poisoning. This turned the skin yellow, giving women the nickname "canaries". Poisoning caused nosebleeds, sickness, dizziness, swollen limbs and even death.

GREATER FREEDOM

Despite the dangers, women flooded into the munitions industries. Compared with other work, particularly domestic service, work in the munitions factories offered better pay and conditions, and greater freedom. Women could also work at night and do housework during the day. As time went on, some protective clothing, nurseries and crèches were introduced.

WOMEN IN MUNITIONS

Most warring countries recruited women munitions workers. Exact numbers are not known. Women in Britain made up a greater percentage of munitions workers than elsewhere. In all cases, women were paid less than men were.

Britain

In 1914 some 212, 000 British women worked in munitions and engineering. By 1918 the figure was nearly one million, accounting for 75 per cent of the labour force.

Germany

Before 1914 the armaments firm, Krupps, employed between 2,000 and 3,000 women. By January 1918, numbers had risen to 28,000. Overall, 700,000 women worked in munitions.

Russia

By 1917 women made up more than 42 per cent of the industrial workforce.

France

Recruitment for women began in 1915. By 1918 women made up 25 per cent of the total munitions labour force.

WORK ON THE LAND

Women also worked on the land. They planted crops, brought in the harvests and kept farms in operation and food supplies flowing. Recruitment varied from country to country, but everywhere women's work on the land was seen as essential.

RECRUITING WOMEN

In Britain, in 1913, only about 117,000 women actually worked on the land. During the war, this number more than doubled. As war dragged on and food shortages began, the British government decided that more women would have to work on farms. They worked with women's voluntary organisations such as the Women's Land Service Corps to recruit women. Some farmers resisted. In 1916 the Board of Trade sent officers around the country to persuade farmers to accept women workers.

Workers of the Women's Land Army help to bring in the harvest in Essex in 1917.

LAND GIRLS

In 1917 the Women's Land Army (WLA) was formed. Girls and young women, mostly from towns, joined in huge numbers. Known as "Land Girls", more than 113,000 women served in the WLA. They did a host of essential tasks, including ploughing, gardening, milking, planting and harvesting. The work was exhausting, hours were long and the life was sometimes lonely. Living accommodation was often basic. Most Land Girls, however, felt it was their patriotic duty to do the work.

"Some people tell me I shall not be able to go on with my farm work in the winter because it will make my hands so bad. Our men don't stop fighting in the cold weather and neither shall I."

Dorothy Chalmers, 1915

MAINLAND EUROPE

The situation was different on mainland Europe; women were not recruited from towns in the same way or in the same numbers. In Italy, France and Russia women continued to work the land as they always had. Their workload increased as they took over the work of absent men. In France, and elsewhere, many women ploughed by hand when the army requisitioned their livestock. In Italy, women preferred to work on the land rather than in the dreadful conditions of the factories.

In Germany food shortages were far worse than in Britain because the Allied naval blockade had cut off food supplies. Nearly 60 per cent of male agricultural workers were called up to serve in the army, so rural women workers were essential. The government tried to recruit women who lived in towns to work on the land, but without success. In 1916 Germany brought in young women from occupied France to do the work. This led to rumours of brutality towards the French women workers, which fuelled anti-German feeling.

☞ WORKING ON THE LAND

Work on the land was difficult and exhausting. Here is an idea of what was expected:

- getting up at 4 am
- milking cows
- feeding pigs and poultry
- planting food crops
- weeding
- threshing
- gathering straw
- picking fruit
- pulling flax for linseed oil
- sleeping on straw mattresses, on wooden frames just off the floor

---

WOMEN'S ORGANISATIONS

In Britain, a number of women's voluntary organisations came into being. They included the Women's Legion, which was launched by the Marchioness of Londonderry in July 1915. By 1917 it had tens of thousands of members. Other organisations included the Women's Institute, still in existence today, the Women's Land Service Corps, the Women's Defence of the Realm Corps and the Women's Volunteer Reserve (WVR). Most were started by upper-class women and each group had their own distinctive uniforms. They worked with the British government to place women in essential war work. Some also raised money and provided services, such as canteens, for soldiers.

WOMEN IN THE FORCES

From 1917 British and American women were enlisted into the armed forces. However, only men went to battle; women were not allowed to fight. There were some exceptions. Flora Sandes fought with forces in Serbia and Russian women fought in the so-called Battalion of Death.

VOLUNTARY ORGANISATIONS

When war began some women wanted to join the military but were not allowed to. In Britain women formed a number of military-style organisations. These included the Women's Emergency Corps and Women's Voluntary Reserve (WVR). They wore khaki uniforms and practised drilling and parading. In Australia women set up the Australian Women's Service Corps.

WOMEN'S SECTIONS

By 1917 there was a serious shortage of soldiers. British women were finally recruited into the forces to free up more men for battle. The Women's Army Auxiliary Corps (WAAC) was set up in 1917. By the end of the year, it employed some 60,000 women, 10,000 of whom served in France. The Women's Royal Naval Service (WRNS) was also created. In 1918 the Women's Royal Air Force (WRAF) developed from the women's arm of the Royal Flying Corps. Women in the forces did not fight, however, and the WRNS remained on land. Nonetheless, women were integrated into the British forces, carried out a host of support duties, wore uniforms and received a salary.

In France the military also used women for a range of work. They remained civilians and were not given military status. When the United States entered the war in 1917, some 13,000 women enlisted in the US Navy, mostly to do clerical work. They were the first women in US history to be admitted to full military rank and status.

"It was awful... we had to get up at about six and do PT (physical training) and march. We drilled in the square and were a laughing stock. We had two weeks' training before we sailed for France."

Ruby Ord describes training in the WAAC

FLORA SANDES

FLORA SANDES (1876-1956) was the only British woman combatant – an extraordinary achievement when even British women who drilled in uniform were mocked. In 1914 Sandes went to Serbia to nurse with the Red Cross. When the Serbs were forced to retreat, Sandes went with them and enlisted as a soldier in the Serbian army. In 1916 she was wounded but, after a spell in hospital, returned to take part in the Serbian victory over the Bulgarians.

WOMEN IN COMBAT

A few individual women did engage in combat. Flora Sandes fought with the Serbian Army and eventually gained the rank of captain. Ecaterina Teodoroiu fought on the Eastern Front with the Romanian army. Killed in action in 1917, she is still a national heroine.

One group of women who actively fought as a group was the Russian "Battalion of Death". In March 1917 the Russian Revolution broke out. Morale among Russian soldiers was low. Maria Botchkareva, a 25-year-old peasant woman, formed a battalion of women "to shame the men". Some 2,000 volunteered. The battalion was given equipment and several male officers as instructors. Three hundred women went to the front where they fought side by side with men. The women fought bravely, suffering heavy casualties, but also taking a number of German prisoners.

☛ AMERICAN WOMEN IN ACTION

American women served in the USA, Europe, Panama, Hawaii, Guam, Puerto Rico, Siberia and Serbia.

◆ The US Navy enrolled some 12,500 women as Yeomen (F), soon known as Yeomanettes.
◆ The US Marine Corps enrolled 300 women.
◆ The US Army employed some 1,300 female civilians for clerical work in the Signal Corps, Quartermasters Corps, Ordnance, Treasury and Secret Service.
◆ More than 200 American women worked for the US Army in Europe as bilingual telephone operators. They were known as the "Hello Girls".

Women soldiers of the Battalion of Death take an oath of loyalty on the old Russian flag in June 1917.

NETWORKS AND SPIES

German forces occupied Belgium and northern France for most of the war. Life for women in occupied territories was hard. Some women resisted while others aided the war effort by helping soldiers to escape, or by acting as spies.

UNDER OCCUPATION

In 1914 German forces pushed into Belgium and northern France. Occupying forces requisitioned homes and supplies, displacing families and leaving them short of supplies such as clothes, fuel and food. German forces recruited women as domestic workers. They had to wash, clean and cook for occupying troops. By 1915 village women were forced to work in the fields, providing food for the forces. During Easter 1916 young French women from Lille, Roubaix and Tourcoing were taken to Germany to work on the land.

NETWORKS

There was little that women in the occupied territories could do to improve their conditions. But some women did resist. They refused to co-operate with German authorities and gave food to prisoners of war. Women in Belgium and France set up secret networks, passing information about troop movements to Allied forces.

Despite the high risk to themselves, women developed networks to help Allied soldiers escape to safety. In 1915 the Germans executed British nurse Edith Cavell. She ran a hospital in Brussels, Belgium, which was part of an escape route. Women in and around Lille, including Louise Thuliez, hid soldiers and took them to Cavell's hospital. From there the soldiers were taken to safety in neutral Holland. Other women in the network included the Comptesse de Belleville and Princess Marie de Croy, who offered her home as a refuge. After the network was discovered, they were sentenced to life imprisonment with hard labour.

✒ WOMEN'S WAR WRITINGS

War stimulated a wealth of writing. Many women wrote about their own experiences. Some women wrote fiction or poetry.

Popular fiction New female heroines were created, based on VADs, munition workers and ambulance drivers. Children's writers, such as Angela Brazil, featured schoolgirls keen "to do their bit" for the war effort.

Poetry Many women wrote poetry. They included: Nancy Cunard, Charlotte Mew, Alice Maynell, Edith Nesbit, Edith Sitwell, Marie Stopes and Katharine Tynan. Unlike men, women did not experience fighting but they too wrote about the horrors of war and the pain of loss and bereavement. Only a few produced patriotic verse. Rose Macaulay wrote poetry and also a celebrated pacifist novel called *Non-Combatants and Others*. It was published in 1916.

Letters and diaries Women from all nations put their thoughts and experiences into letters and diaries. Some have been published and give a clear insight into women's war experiences. One of the best known is *Testament of Youth* by Vera Brittain.

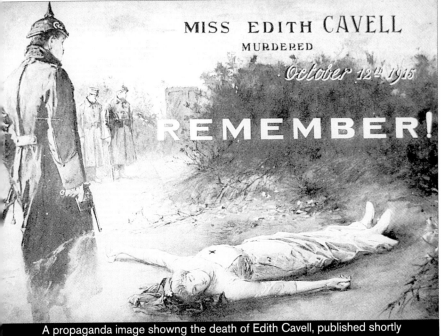

MISS EDITH CAVELL
MURDERED
October 12th 1915

REMEMBER!

A propaganda image showing the death of Edith Cavell, published shortly after her execution.

SPIES

Another woman who also helped soldiers and spied for the Allies was Louise de Bettignies. Working in occupied France, she passed information back to British intelligence. In October 1915 she and her colleague, Marie-Léonie Vanhoutte, were captured. They escaped execution, but Bettignies died in prison in 1918.

Other women too worked as spies. Marthe Richer, also known as Marthe Richard, was a French aviator. She was based in Spain and worked as a double agent, passing on information that she obtained from a German officer, with whom she had a relationship.

The best-known female spy was probably Mata Hari (Margaretha Zella MacLeod). In 1916 French intelligence recruited her to spy for France. She was instructed to seduce the Crown Prince of Germany and gain information. Instead she arrived in Spain, where she formed a relationship with a German officer. She passed on information, thinking she was working for French intelligence. The French, however, believed she was spying for Germany. When she returned to France in 1917, she was arrested and executed.

"I realise that patriotism is not enough. I must have no hatred or bitterness towards anyone."

Edith Cavell's last words before being shot, 12 October 1915

WOMEN FOR PEACE

Not all women supported the war. Some were deeply opposed, and in 1915 a women's peace congress met at The Hague. At first pacifists were just ridiculed, but from 1916 onwards they were persecuted and imprisoned.

EARLY VOICES

When war broke out, some women, including feminists and socialists, were horrified. Sylvia Pankhurst said war was a "huge and shameful loss to humanity". In August 1914, 1,500 women marched for peace in New York, and a national Women's Peace Party (WPP) emerged. By 1915 an international women's peace movement had been founded based on the International Women's Suffrage Alliance (IWSA).

ROSIKA SCHWIMMER

ROSIKA SCHWIMMER (1877-1948) was a tireless pacifist and feminist. In 1913 she became secretary of the International Woman's Suffrage Alliance (IWSA). In 1915 she helped to form the US Women's Peace Party and to set up the Women's Peace Congress.

After the Congress she went to London, Berlin, Vienna, Budapest, Rome, Berne and Paris to speak to governments about ending the war. In 1919 she became vice-president of the Women's International League for Peace and Freedom (WILPF).

WOMEN'S PEACE CONGRESS

In 1914 Dutch feminist Aletta Jacobs, Hungarian Rosika Schwimmer and American feminist Jane Addams called for "Women of All Nations" to gather at The Hague in neutral Holland. Some 1,150 women from 12 nations responded to the call.

The Congress met between 28 April and 1 May 1915. It was a remarkable achievement, bringing together women from both neutral and warring nations. Press and governments were hostile and tried to prevent women attending. Most of the British women delegates were not allowed travel permits. The North Sea was closed to shipping; only three British women arrived. The German government stopped all but 28 women from crossing the border. French and Russian feminists boycotted the Congress.

Jane Addams chaired the Congress. Its aim was to mediate for peace and find ways of preventing future wars. Following the Congress, 30 women delegates went to heads of state to demand an end to war.

The Congress was unable to stop the war. But by November 1915, there were peace groups in 11 European countries, seven of which were at war. The Women's International League for Peace and Freedom (WILPF) resulted from the Congress. It still exists today.

PERSECUTION

From 1916 attitudes towards pacifists hardened. People saw them as unpatriotic and treacherous. They were accused of betraying men at the front. Women – and men – who spoke against the war took great risks.

In France the Sûreté drew up a list of known anti-war activists, and a leading activist, Louise Saumoneau, was arrested. In Germany activists Rosa Luxembourg and Clara Zetkin were imprisoned.

In Britain some women joined the No Conscription Fellowship to help conscientious objectors escape internment. Some, such as Nellie Best and Alice Wheeler, were arrested and mistreated. When America entered the war in 1917, President Woodrow Wilson declared that pacifists were disloyal citizens. It became an offence to speak, write or organise against the war. As a result, only a few women, including anarchist Emma Goldman, continued anti-war activities.

Women Against War
1914

July International Women's Suffrage Alliance (IWSA) calls on governments not to go to war.

August Women in suffrage movement split over whether to support war.

August Women's Peace March takes place in New York.

1915

Socialist women against the war meet in Berne, Switzerland.

January More than 3,000 women attend a meeting in Washington. They form the Women's Peace Party.

28 April–1 May International Women's Peace Congress meets "to protest against war and to suggest steps which may lead to warfare becoming an impossibility." [Aletta Jacobs]. Peace groups are set up in many European countries.

1916

No Conscription Fellowship is formed in Britain.

1917

America enters the war. Emma Goldman co-founds the No Conscription League, but most anti-war protest dies away.

1917–18

In Germany and Russia, women protest against economic hardship and mounting casualties. Some women demand an end to war.

1919

Women's International League for Peace and Freedom (WILPF) is set up. It remains active today.

The photograph on the opposite page shows the American delegation to the International Women's Peace Conference at The Hague in 1915.

THE HOME FRONT

World War One affected all aspects of women's daily lives. Women and children experienced food shortages and suffered from bombing. By 1917 women in many countries were protesting against the effects of war.

HARDSHIPS

It was difficult for women to manage work and families during the war years and many suffered economic hardships. In Britain, France and Germany soldiers' wives received a small allowance from the state but it was often not enough to live on.

Both Britain and Germany set up naval blockades to stop food being imported into each other's country. There were food shortages in Britain, but food production remained good. Women queued for food but rationing was not introduced until January 1918.

Germany suffered dreadfully from the blockade and food shortages were severe. Even turnips, acorns and horse chestnuts were rationed. In Russia, women struggled to survive on the lowest wages in Europe.

AIR RAIDS

In August 1914 Germany bombed Paris. Air raids – by zeppelins and later aeroplanes – continued throughout the war, mainly on Britain. A new phrase – the "Home Front" – entered the language to describe the fact that civilians, like soldiers, were also fighting the war. Women gained a reputation for calmness and heroism. But bombing took its toll. Some women suffered "air-raid shock" – similar to the shellshock suffered by men in the trenches.

PROTEST AND WEARINESS

By and large women's morale in Britain remained high, but there were some protests. In 1915 women in Glasgow took to the streets in protest when authorities tried to evict a soldier's family after their rent was raised.

SYLVIA PANKHURST

SYLVIA PANKHURST (1882-1960) was a suffragette and pacifist. During the war she worked with needy mothers and children in London's East End. She set up low-cost restaurants and created a toy factory to provide work for unemployed women. She also took over a pub – renamed the Mother's Arms – and used it for a day nursery, clinic and school. Through her newspaper, *Workers Dreadnought*, she exposed working conditions in the munitions factories and called for food distribution through the state.

"Another very bad Zeppelin raid on London & district on Wednesday night. About 50 people were killed."

Vera Brittain's diary, October 1915

This British poster encouraged civilians to avoid waste and help the war effort.

Elsewhere, women's protests were becoming increasingly bitter and desperate. In France, women workers demonstrated for better wages as early as 1915. In Germany women protested against food shortages and high prices.

By 1917 the war had reached crisis point. Many people thought it would never end. In Russia, soldiers mutinied and women demanded an end to the fighting. On 8 March 1917 – International Women's Day – a women's food march heralded the start of the Russian Revolution. Some months later, Russia left the war.

Life On The "Home Front"

1914

30 August German aircraft bomb Paris.

21 December German air raid takes place over Dover.

1915

January First German zeppelin raid on Britain.

February Britain and Germany announce naval blockades.

Late February Protests over rising prices in London and food shortages in Berlin.

Late May Women protest against food shortages in Berlin and Trieste.

June Women's Rent Strike takes place in Glasgow.

September Women's Co-operative Guild reports on poverty and maternity.

October German women protest against high food prices.

1916

January German zeppelins raid Paris and England.

June French women munitions workers go on strike.

1917

January Women workers strike in Paris and Leeds.

February German women demonstrate against food shortages.

8 March "February Revolution" in Russia follows women's food riots.

May Women workers strike in France.

June Daylight bombing raids on London do extensive damage.

1918

February Meat and fats are rationed in Britain.

August Maternity and Child Welfare Act in Britain enables local authorities to provide welfare clinics and health visitors.

THE END OF WAR

On 11 November 1918, World War One finally ended. The war had involved women in ways no other war had ever done before, but the question as to how much it changed women's lives is complex.

LIBERATING WOMEN?

It is sometimes said World War One "liberated" women from their homes. This is not quite accurate. Total war meant that women were mobilised as never before and in every kind of job, much of it so-called "men's work".

But when war ended, war industries closed. Returning servicemen went back to work and women were dismissed or barred from most jobs. Women were encouraged back into the home as wives and mothers or into "traditional" working roles. But war work had given women confidence and new experiences. Many working-class girls refused to go back into domestic service. Ultimately, patterns of work changed.

WAGES AND WELFARE

During the war, more women joined trade unions. In England and Wales, women's trade union membership rose from 357,000 in 1914 to 1,086,000 in 1918. Women's incomes rose but they still earned less than men, and the fight for equal pay would continue until the 1970s.

War brought changes in welfare too. Many women were left widowed or single, and children were left without fathers. In Britain, Germany and the USA, welfare provision and family allowances were introduced to help mothers and children.

POLITICAL GAINS

One major change was that women in many countries finally gained the vote. There is debate, however, over whether women gained the vote because of their war work or would have done so anyway.

"… before… my twenty-first birthday, I had experienced the deaths of my father, my brother, my favourite school friend and the husband to whom I had been married for five weeks."

Baroness Barbara Wootton

KÄTHE KOLLWITZ

Käthe Kollwitz (1867-1945) was a German artist and sculptor. Her youngest son, Peter, was killed in battle in October 1915. The tragedy deeply affected her life and influenced her work. For many years she worked on a granite monument of her son, which also showed his grieving parents. In 1932 it was installed as a war memorial at Diksmuide, Flanders, where it stands today. Writing in her diaries of the war, she said: "There has been enough of dying! Let not another man fall."

The British government began discussing reform of the franchise as early as 1916. Suffrage leaders such as Millicent Fawcett reminded the government of the work that women were doing, and insisted political reform had to include women. Finally, in 1918 British women gained the vote and the right to elect women MPs. The franchise only applied to propertied women over 30, but it was a start. In 1928 the vote was extended to women over 21, on equal terms with men.

EXHAUSTION AND GRIEF

Women greeted the end of war with relief. Some celebrated but many were too weary to take part; most women had lost at least one male relative or friend. Women had also died. Some women were determined that such a war should never be repeated and worked for peace. Some created memorials for the fallen. Britain, France and other nations raised monuments to the women who had died during the war.

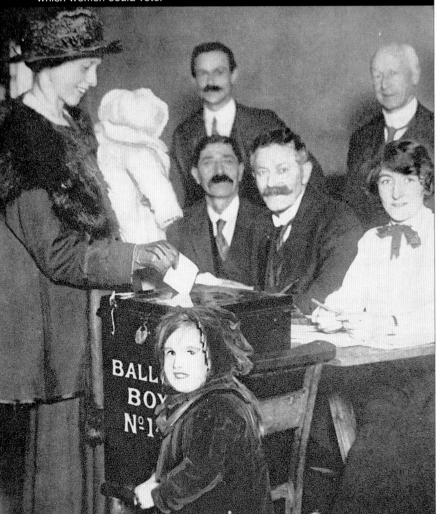

The British General Election of 14 December 1918 was the first in which women could vote.

GLOSSARY

Allies Britain and its colonies, France, Russia and other nations, including the USA, who fought against Germany in World War One.

Amputation Surgical removal of a limb or part of a limb.

"Canary girls" Name given to female British munitions workers who suffered jaundice through handling TNT and other chemical poisons. Their skin turned a bright yellow colour.

Clearing station A makeshift hospital or area where casualties from the battlefield were initially treated before being moved farther back away from the front.

Conscription Compulsory enlistment into the army or other armed service.

Conscientious objector Someone who refuses to fight for reasons of conscience. During World War One many were imprisoned and treated badly. Some conscientious objectors took part in the war effort by driving ambulances.

Crèche A day nursery for babies and young children.

FANYs First-Aid Nursing Yeomanry. Formed in 1907 as a link between frontline fighting units and field hospitals. FANYs sometimes called themselves the "First Anywheres".

Feminist A person who promotes women's rights.

Field hospital A hospital set up near to the battlefield, often in a tent, marquee, church hall or abandoned building.

Front line Where two opposing armies face each other.

Gangrene Dead or decomposing body tissue.

Home Front A term that appeared during World War One to take into account and acknowledge the work that civilians at home did for the war effort. It was used to illustrate the fact that home life too was affected by war.

Internment To be confined or imprisoned, usually for a certain period.

IWSA International Women's Suffrage Alliance. An association of the main women's suffrage organisations in member nations.

Militant War-like.

Mobilise To prepare an army for war. Governments also mobilised civilians for the war effort, particularly women.

Munitions Armaments.

No-man's-land Area between two opposing armies, which is not controlled by either army. Wounded soldiers often fell in no-man's-land and either had to crawl back to their line or be collected, often under fire.

NUWSS National Union of Women's Suffrage Societies. The largest British women's suffrage society. Founded in 1897.

Pacifist A person who is opposed to war and violence.

Recruit A person who joins the army or other armed service voluntarily.

Suffragette A woman who fought for the vote using militant methods, including breaking the law. The *Daily Mail* first used the word in 1906 to describe the "unladylike" tactics of the Women's Social and Political Union (WSPU).

Suffragist A person who campaigned for the right to vote, using peaceful, law-abiding methods. The word comes from "suffrage", meaning the right to vote.

VADs Voluntary Aid Detachments. British uniformed voluntary nursing service. First created in 1909 to provide medical assistance during wartime.

WSPU Women's Social and Political Union. British women's suffrage society founded in 1903. Members were known as suffragettes.

Voluntary work Unpaid work. A volunteer is someone who chooses to do something without the certainty of being paid.

INDEX